Caribou Planet

Gary Lawless

Thanks to the editors, publishers, translators and friends, for the many opportunities for my poems to find their ways out into the world.

This selection is for the animals.

Front cover art by Stephen Petroff

Ice Tattoo art by Stephen Petroff

Sitka Spring art by Li Ching Accurso

Cuban Heart art by Richard Lee

Sardine Shards by Kimberly Callas

Common Ground photo by Roger Leisner

Back cover photo "In Croatia" by Beth Leonard

ISBN: 978 0 982438 99 2

Copyright Gary Lawless, 2015

Blackberry Books

617 East Neck Road

Nobleboro, Maine   04555

chimfarm@gwi.net

When the animals come to us,

    asking for our help,

    will we know what they are saying?

When the plants speak to us

    in their delicate, beautiful language,

    will we be able to answer them?

When the planet herself

    sings to us in our dreams

    will we be able to wake ourselves, and act?

Treat each bear as the last bear.

Each wolf the last, each caribou.

Each track the last track.

Gone spoor, gone scat.

There are no more deer trails,

no more flyways.

Treat each animal as sacred,

each minute our last.

Ghost hooves. Ghost skulls.

Death rattles and

dry bones.

Each bear walking alone

in warm night air.

You are the last whale,

washed up on a far beach.

The waves are pushing against you,

pushing against you.

Your brothers and sisters are gone.

The light is too bright for your eyes.

You cannot breath.

Small children are throwing rocks and laughing,

climbing onto your body

You die alone, your ears full of wind.

You are the last buffalo.

The sun is setting over the plains.

You stand alone, enormous,

heavy with fur, lonely.

You are tired of running,

tired of running.

All of your friends have gone.

It seems even the earth has turned against you.

There is no one to say goodbye.

You rest, listening to the wind.

When the time is right,

the spirit of the wolf returns.

Yellow Dog   (for Yozo)

Will I discover the yellow dog who lives

within the sunlit garden

of your body, breathing deep

water like old cave walls,

spirals of moisture and aged stone?

Will I discover the hidden passage,

the lost and forgotten tunnel –

How marvelous to find

a wall of muscled flesh,

how wonderful these beasts, how soft,

as if I had crawled through

the labyrinth of rock to

come upon a garden of sinew

in the lush bloom of pelt,

all moving in spirals toward

the chambered ceiling, torches flickering.

Smoke carries magic.

Will I discover a cave of light,

animals dancing in the bloodied

sheath of our lives?

(Yellow Dog…)

I do not want to be separate from your name.

I do not want to be separate from your skin.

We travel the walled lines of your maze,

remembering corners, leaving pieces of ourselves

as clues for the return passage.

Deep pools of fur.

I close my eyes,

close my eyes and see

animals dancing on walls

deep within us

just beyond the light,

flickering.

Little by little

roads eat away the hearts of mountains.

Fires burn through,

come back in huckleberries.

Trails close in August, too many bears.

Too many bears,

now following avalanche chutes,

Glacier lily, early spring.

Caribou in old growth spruce,

Lichen, banks of

snow and fog.

Bear tracks in the mud.

Close the roads.

Every stump is sacred.

Every stump a saint.

Every silted river a church to which

the pilgrim salmon return.

Every breath of wind a love song.

We worship in wetlands,

bow to the fern, the rock,

the holy salamander.

The blood of sweet water.

The body of moss.

Eel Grass, Sears Island

Hard to be lonely

in the lushness of

Eel grass, feeling the ocean's

ebb and flow –

hard to know

want or hurt or

waste, here below

the sun, the sky,

the water's edge of

grass and mud and

moving with the moon –

hard to know

the hearts of men, those

who would fill and spill and

kill all below

their own shallow depth of heart, their

line of sight –

hard to know these hearts,

hard to be alive,

(Eel Grass…)

hard to survive

in the face of their

rush toward riches,

toward death,

hard to be alive.

For those who would compromise the forest

The spirits of the lost trees,

the spirits of the plants,

the moss spirits, the rock spirits

consign you to a hell of

no birds, a dry spare hell where

your name will not be known –

you will be known as desolation,

ruiner of planets, the lonely soul who

lives without the friendship of life,

without the solace of species –

the ghosts of those you have

pushed aside will follow you as

you move toward dryness, dust, and empty skies –

Surely goodness and mercy will

leave your wretched life untouched

as you dwell forever in

a land without life,

trying to remember the sound

of birds, the sound of wind,

the sound of your own heart, beating.

The good news

Roads disappear, and the caribou wander through.

The beaver gets tired of it, reaches

up, through the ice,

grabs the trappers feet and

pulls him down.

Wolves come back on their own,

circle the State House,

howl at the sportswriters and

piss on the ATVs.

Trees grow everywhere.

The machines stop,

and the air is full of birdsong.

We ride the old winds

    Carry our song from place to place

    Carry our song from place to place

One dream, one people

    One story to tell

Watch light in the eye

    From face to face

Light in the eye

    From face to face.

Labrador South

I

Dark skies, silver slices of fish in the tide,

the lights of Labrador, across the Strait,

men with long-handled nets dip caplin

from the surf, bait

for tomorrow's traps.

At the stage, piles of fish, long knives,

blood of the trout

blood of the cod

dead seal and flatfish

wind and scud ice

George goes to feed the pig.

II

Whales chase the caplin onto the beaches,

humpback and finback, just offshore.

The moose is lying in the snow.

Rock ptarmigan bathing in mud

The waves are breaking against me

The net, full of fish, has lost its bottom.

Peat is burning, the wind full of smoke.

Cod at my feet, wide-eyed in death.

The moon, just rising, over the mountains.

III

Five of us in the cab of the truck,

the bed full of cod.

Skies a dark blue, fires on the beach.

Lighthouse walls seven feet thick, no wind.

Freighters slide by.

An iceberg caught in the nets,

caught in a cod trap, five boatloads of fish.

No freeboard in black water.

Cut out the cod's tongue.

Brooks tumbling from summit tables

thickets of coarse herbs and low shrubs

tangles as high as your head

Ladies Mantle a misty fringe

at the edge of falling water

Looking for Rivers

Looking for rivers. The stones are full of

light. Bright water. He rubbed the leaves

between his hands, flew above the trees.

I followed, thanked him. This at Piccadilly Head.

Where the road ends. Green leaves on a slender

branch. The Mass, still in French. Sheep in the road,

again. A yard full of bones. How many dogs. How

many footprints, in the snow.

Moonlight, fish scale, ice diamonds. Lifting

my arms from the sea, the water, falling around me,

let loose from nets and lines, shining as it falls.

My hands to the sky, handlining the depths.

I am the wind which blows over the sea.

I am a wave of the sea.

Too many voices, whispering. Too many

directions, too many words for snow. Words rub

against my skin like wind, words piled over my

head like stones. Each sound carries news. Songs

come to me in dreams. Birds speak as they fly

overhead. Everything speaks. We live an uninterrupted

conversation of life and light, light

filtering through the stones, through the fog,

gleaming off ice, warming fur, warming skin.

Sometimes I hear voices, I dream.

Sometimes I don't know if I'm caribou or

whale, man or woman, sometimes I don't

know but I'm the whole damn thing, ocean,

trees and sky - I

came down a raven and I danced upon the earth.

I came down a raven and I danced upon the earth.

There's lots I forget. Songs I've known so well.

I forget them. In my day it was all songs

and stories. You'd get in a house and someone

would sing a song, then someone else would sing.

All kinds of songs. All those songs had

stories, good songs about storms, women,

murder on board ship, hard times. There was

always a song for hard times. That's all

you had to do to pass the time. It went from

one to the other, and what you didn't know,

you made up. I was never real good at it, but

the old folks used to know some songs...

"Now you might think I'm goofy

but the man in the moon is a Newfy.

He's sailing home to glory

in a great big silver dory."

We fished out of dories then. It was all

dories and nets, jigs and handlines. We didn't have

motors then. The wind....

I like to sit on the steps, feel the wind,

see the birds, smell the ocean. I don't like it

when I'm inside. I don't feel connected

to anything. I feel like I'm missing something,

like something is happening, without me.

Beth just painted the steps blue. I like to

sit out there, listen and wait. I like to feel

like I'm part of something.

Ain't it lonely when it rains, water on wood,

Ain't it sad.

My arms are tired of fish, nets and oars,

my shoulders ache, my hips, my hands are tired

of cold water, rope, the movements of the knife,

my eyes are tired of light off water, off ice,

watching down lines, staring into snow, I want to

be covered with water. I want to drown in my

sleep, the light disappearing, overhead, birds

diving down, into the darkness, I want to drown

in my sleep.

You break the surface, break the surface and

fall through into some new kind of light.

Last night the moon came up red.

The dogs were barking.

At dusk the sky was full of birds.

I kept thinking about

all of the places I've never been.

"snow walker"

Lines of smoke

now vertical, now to the southwest.

Old brush and last year's wood.

Hunted the caribou, until they were gone.

Cod and salmon, whales tore up the nets.

His last words:

"What's all that barking?"

Dogs gone to meet strangers,

entering the village.

Orion the mighty

hunter of winter,

early in the evening.

Spirits descending.

Walking the earth in coats of fur.

Walking the earth in coats of fur.

Moving along the Milky Way and down,

darkness surrounds,

awake in the woods,

Walking the earth in coats of fur.

Bear walking north, following glaciers.

Fresh green valleys, the land rising, falling.

Flocks of birds overhead.

Berries and mushrooms.

Gatherings on river banks,

Pawing at salmon resting in shallows.

Sunlight and salt wind,

wind in our fur,

sun on our backs,

on our backs in

fresh green grass,

walking north.

After the ground dried

we tasted ice in the meat of animals

for a long time.

Berries grew but never ripened.

The mountains moved slowly

away from us.

Who can say what anything means?

We watch as the leaves turn color.

Fish come again to the streams,

spawn, and are gone.

It has always been important to us

that the caribou move freely,

that the grasses return each spring,

the water, running to the sea.

We split open the rocks.

There were faces inside.

What were they saying?

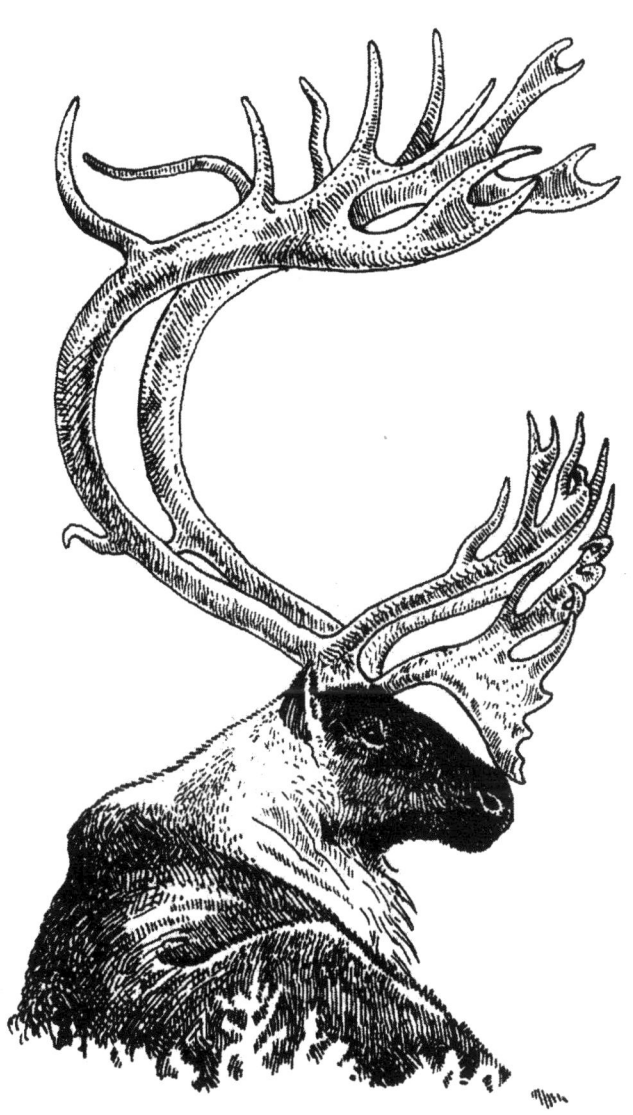

Caribou Man

He went there in a dream,

to the place where the caribou go,

to the mountain where the caribou go,

mountain not of snow, but of caribou hair.

He became the Caribou Man,

came to live among them,

eating moss, fathering young,

riding on the backs of the bulls.

He gives meat to the hunters.

He takes care of the caribou.

"In a dream she came, she called me.

She stepped from the herd,

whispered my name,

Come live as husband

among the caribou."

We talked with him,

wishing meat for our families.

He warned that our troubles came

from killing too freely.

We must kill only for food,

(Caribou Man…)

To renew tools, tents and clothing.

We must not waste life.

Their blood is his blood.

Their blood is our blood.

Their dreams are our dreams and he

is one of us.

Charred antler as star sign.

Borne into the house of ice,

passing through the doorway

of the breath of flesh, suspended.

The dream opens out into

flat space, land scarred, carved,

ridge and valley, glacial trails the

ice tattoo, carried

within us.

We came down for the singing,

the feasting and the wine, the dancing ...

We had no idea.

The pink flesh of salmon, smoke from cedar fires,

days by the river, the sun over the mountains,

the bogs, thick with berries,

soft birds rising through early morning mist ...

We had no idea, really.

We wanted to come home saying

                  "It was a wonderful time.

                  We had great fun."

More than what I've got

is to enter spirit

world split open,

animals migrate through me,

cross the river, fly

home.

Bad feelings and smoke.

Something about the color of ice:

Jagged, pale blue.

The direction of the wind.

Spirits walk the snow. The walls of the house

have voices of their own. Everything is alive.

Fallen antlers rise at night and walk

in procession. The dead rise and visit the living.

Birds fly through smoke, changing colors.

When the men returned, they killed the sled dogs,

hung them from poles. We were afraid.

If given the choice,

dropping this body for another.

Wolves somewhere on the edges of light,

waiting for the weak.

waiting for us to fall.

I will leave this body.

I will feed the wolves.

I will journey home.

Caribouddhism

1

The iceberg has come

to speak with Nanao.

She is just beyond the window,

waiting beyond the light.

She has come a long way.

She has a message for us.

She is very shy.

If we look directly at her

She begins to melt away,

All that she

has to say, lost

to the light of

day, the wind, the

rocks, our eyes –

She begins to speak.

We must listen

very carefully.

2

Tonight she comes as

moose, no longer iceberg,

tiptoeing carefully

between the tents.

She is happy in darkness.

She is looking for Nanao.

She wants to enter

his dreams.

3

Today she is standing

beside the road

in a patch of bog and

dirty snow.

She is the color of glacier,

iceberg, snow and

light.

She turns and

disappears,

into the woods.

She is caribou,

She is iceberg,

She is message,

and dream.

Twillingate/Terra Nova/Gros Morne

Newfoundland

Caribou Sutra

We learn to be tender

with each other.

We learn to turn

and wait.

We cannot walk

alone for long.

We take our songs

out of the air,

speak the language of

sun on the rocks

at the edge of the river.

We learn when to cross,

when to return.

Let us be blessed with birds.

Let us remember the sound

    of wings in still air,

      songs in early morning sunlight.

Let us carve beautiful birds,

send our souls to fly away.

    Let us carve beautiful birds,

    send our souls to fly away.

SITKA

SPRING

First thing I hear

      Ravens (Old Grandfather)

Sitka spruce, ancient cedar,

raven, duck, bald eagle.

I want to open myself to them all,

hear what they have to say.

      Learning to breathe with ducks.

      Learning to speak with raven.

"We don't say anything bad about the animals"

The bear had put her in a trance.

The shaman saw their tracks, followed them.

Snowy mountain slopes in sunlight,

harbor under cloud.

sea lions and gulls

mark the passage of herring.

Raven calls from a nearby tree.

Things are done to keep balance.

Ken drives the jeep to Halibut Point.

We eat smoked salmon, watching the ocean.

Herring spawn has turned the water

milky white.

Hundreds of gulls gather, bald

eagles in treetops, sea lions, ravens.

Three humpbacks swim through,

close to shore.

We dip our hands in the water,

gather the delicate eggs,

taste the seed of the sea.

After days of sitting on

driftwood beach rock,

birds too numerous to count,

watching for eagle,

listening for raven,

now, even though it is cold,

now, even though the wind is wet,

I begin to leave the ground.

Li wants to know

where the birds go

when it rains.

Out by the pulp mill

the harbor seals swim

in the effluent.

Log booms

skim the foam.

Trout rises for a fly.

Out on the horizon

the volcano sits,

quiet.

Return the bones to moving water

moving water like prayers

prayers like colored ribbons

among the trees

prayers like the bird you hear,

but can't see

prayers like moving water

return the bones, like prayers

Trying to find the language

of ravens,

We are late for the tide,

late for mass, late for the

sunrise, late for the mountain –

The trails are covered with snow,

or fast moving water, wind –

Language falls from treetops,

from nets pulled up from the

bottom – a raven feather on

the rock – a shell in your

hand – something flies over –

conversation drifts

Suddenly alive,

Raven brings me back.

Lulled by the water, duck talk,

mountains reaching

into my heart,

the bridge of dreams,

the snow-covered life.

Raven's voice pulls me back,

awake, tells me:

"You pay attention!

If you want to hear the story

      put your hands in the water

If you want to hear the story

      watch where the wind carries us."

Which World

There is a path,

winding between Sitka spruce,

passing totem poles stolen

from their island homes,

emptied of ash and bone,

placed along the trail.

In the distance, a volcano.

Raven flies

just above the surface of things, bald

eagle watching through layers of air and water

for the fish

passing through

shining in the cold

river like light

from another world.

Everything moving, everything

moving to

come together, come together and

(Which World…)

fall apart, again.

The water rushing.

The heart beating.

I am waiting for you

at the mouth of the river.

Host Rock

Isle Royale National Park

Lake Superior

Isle Royale

A place where the wolves are wanted,

where human beings bring our awkward blessings

to moose bone, wolf scat, loon song,

where we allow ourselves to blossom

among marsh marigold, rock harlequin,

Calypso orchid, Labrador tea.

Where we peel back layers of fog, moss, rock itself –

Inside there is sunlight

Inside there is wolf song

the light step of the moose,

berries waiting to ripen

where the light never touches –

all this light

at the heart of things.

Paddling home after the poetry reading,

10 PM and an hour to travel.

The sun has just gone down,

leaving us beautiful light.

The lake is flat.

There is no breeze.

Beaver slaps his tail.

Various ducks and loons let us know –

Once we hear human voices and see

a lantern, in a cabin window

behind the islands –

Let it get no darker

Let it stay this calm

and we will travel all night,

longer, into this peace of

land and sky, coming together

somewhere, just beyond us.

Water connects with water.

Six days with little rain.

The moose is in the swamp.

Ducks begin to speak.

We walk the ridgelines

thirsty for everything:

that yellow flower,

that bird overhead -

Without knowing, we drink,

leave with the island

inside of us.

Layer upon layer of leaves

settles slowly,

moss growing on top.

Layer upon layer of lava flow,

minerals rising to fill the veins.

Burned bare ridges and parallel bogs.

As we walk our minds

drop layer upon layer

down to host rock:

tough, bare, essential.

The wind can't harm us.

The water, all around,

touches, touches,

waiting for the glacier.

I'm scared of the glacier.

It's coming back, I'm sure of it –

It's been here before, several times –

It was cold this morning.

I'm sure I saw ice in the cove.

Are all the birds flying away?

Everything seems to have fur.

Is that fog?

Are you sure that's fog?

Walking home at 10 PM,

night before the solstice full moon,

very pleasant walk to my

cabin hermitage when

Oh no! a hell of

candy wrappers, toilet paper and

one two three four times

"Jeff and Theresa"

scratched into the rock –

May they die alone,

never seeing each other again, in a

swamp where their bones are

never found, not even

by the wolves –

We are an unwanted, introduced species.

For the Earth Watchers

The bones of the saints

are carried from the cedar swamps

by pilgrims who return, year after year,

to seek out the holy sites of departure.

Here the moose spirit

has left its host rock.

How we lie down

sweet and hungry.

Every beautiful morning of the world

I choose the fog

I choose the wolf

I choose to learn to walk again

on moss with the moose through

water in air,

water under foot,

breathing the breath of the world

on every beautiful morning.

Nothing but moosetrails in the mist,

today's fog and wind,

trees against sky.

I want to disappear into cloud,

wander my way to sunlight,

follow the moose down

secret trails in the woods

to reach the places where the wolves

rest upon the ridges, within us,

where the heart wanders, wild.

Deep inside the

rock becoming

fossil –

No longer here –

The wind keeps moving,

moose go on their way,

birds land, and leave –

clouds, fog, sunny days –

Everything sinking, slowly

into stone –

Comes the day and we're gone

(no longer visible –

      -harder and down-)

These gifts the island gives:

the moose swimming across the harbor

the moon rising above fog

flowers along the trail

the sweet gift of birdsong you

can't wait for the island to come to you –

The gifts are given without warning.

You must be there watching, listening,

and the gift must move like water –

You must pass it on

in whatever way you fashion.

INVITO venerdì 22 ottobre, ore 2030

a scuolar dei salmoni

con

GARY LAWLESS

CARIBOUDDISM

poeta bioregionalista

dal Gulf of Maine Bioregion U.S.A.

FESTA POETICA con rinfresco Vegetariano

Associazione Culturale   - CONTRIBUTO L. 7000 -

"ARCOBALENO FIAMMEGGIANTE" vico s. pietro d majella 6 (p.za Bellini) NAPOLI

Relics

Once it was Saint Anthony's

tongue in Padua, Claire's body in

Assisi, bone fragments and

pieces of the True Cross.

Now there are remnant

lowland forest relic

coastal wetlands, turtles

in sunlight, egrets, coots,

pine, beech, mushrooms

and the last few bears –

The blood turned liquid,

rich green moving water,

saints and holy places,

listening to the voice of the owl

in the dark night.

(for Maurizio and Elena)

If, in Montefalco, I cannot say

that I have you in my heart,

do not be alarmed.

Here Santa Chiara announced

that she had manifested the

True Cross, in her heart.

The Church, not taken with

metaphor, cut open her

body, searching her heart

for evidence of the Cross.

They now display,

600 years later,

her dark and fragile body.

Above it, cut open and

dried, her heart, and the

three gallstones,

announced as representing

The Holy Trinity,

Father, Son and Spirit —

In this town

I dare not speak

what is in my heart.

Black birds lifting from ploughed ground,

rows of olives,

crossing the Tiber on the Roman road,

the mountains behind us.

Community of the hilltop, river, valley,

Community of stone

Community of air where

white doves fly

to the mouth of the cave.

For the Po

A land given milk by the wolf,

Francis, taking the paw,

Gubbio and its hillside churchyard –

These old sacred lands where

the pawprint is faint indeed –

We listen in vain for the songbird,

search long for the bear, end by

wandering along the flat river,

Po to the sea, bird refuge,

poison water – somewhere

voices lifted, wolf song,

birdsong, singing back

the milk of the land,

the faint, holy

voices by the river.

Saint Lucy, Venice

Gondola sunset

pink to the Dolomites

limestone sky

where the walk

ends in water we

wet our feet

pray to Saint Lucy

to go, to see -

Where am I and what matter,

in this town, Gubbio,

where the skies clear,

where the wolf lies

buried in the churchyard –

where streets slope the hillside into rain

where in the painting the little dog

far down in the lower corner

on the edge of the crowd

lifts his paw to Francis

like his brother wolf

like her sister wolf –

A whispering in the heart, the place

where we walk, together,

where tablets rise from ploughed ground this

fertile earth, this lasting metallic

taste of language, just there

at the tips of our tongues, where

we raise our hands,

to Francis, to Gubbio, to

not knowing where we are,

and the clouds part, wherever.

For Etain

Goddess among olives.

Goddess of mulberry, and grape.

Goddess of the hearth.

Epona the horse goddess.

Goddess of donkeys.

I come as a wildman,

in the company of wolves.

I touch the land, and bless it,

where no man is turned away,

and our prayers are the sweet songs

of talk around the table.

Leading donkeys to apples in

a warm Umbrian valley where

Francis, turned away from the abbey,

walked the valley toward Assisi-

It all seems so simple, and beautiful:

apples and hay for the horses,

grapes, olives, the last sunlight

along the ridgeline –

with our hearts open, the whole world

walking the valley, toward Assisi.

I won't give my heart to Saint Francis,

but to these hills, his hills,

or any hills where

wolves have walked, where

songbirds sing the day

as common as dirt,

as necessary as water –

Here lightning entered the earth

Here the moon rose, over the lake –

As we walk to the sibyl's cave

music fills the air.

Ice Man Sutra –

    Bolzano

Where everything is revealed.

These are the mountains.

These are the mountains

    beyond the mountains.

This is the sky.

This is the sky

    beyond the sky.

This is the moment

    beyond the mountains

    beyond the sky.

FESTA della
MADRE TERRA
mercoledì 14 ottobre, ore 20.00
OSPITE D'ONORE
GARY LAWLESS
POETA BIOREGIONALISTA
americano
POESIA
MUSICA
cena
Vegetariana
contributo associativo L.20.000

a cura di
RETE BIOREGIONALE ITALIANA
EVALUNA LABORATORIO di SCRITTURA CREATIVA
Associazione Culturale "ARCOBALENO FIAMMEGGIANTE"
vico s. pietro a majella 6, Napoli, tel. 081-455026

In Napoli where our hearts

were sheltered by the rainbow.

In Napoli where the reporter

told us there is no nature

In Napoli where the blood

turns liquid, bringing us luck.

 Napoli where the volcano

Napoli where the sea

Napoli where the singers

Napoli where the living and the dead

In Napoli where we walk

In Napoli where the sun

In Napoli where

Our hearts

The bears are riding scooters

    in Napoli.

Wolves are shopping for neckties

    fancy underwear and maybe

    leather pants.

Wild boars are carrying cell phones but

    no one knows what to say.

We are the advance guard

    of an ancient civilization,

    ashes in our mouths.

The dead are everywhere.

(for Beth)

In Sicily I want to

eat and drink and

walk along the shore with

my arm around you,

and fall asleep happy.

Which is more beautiful,

the volcano or

the Greek column,

in ruins?

Who cares if we've had too much wine –

We are walking toward Tunis,

there are temples on the ridgeline,

and the wind tastes like sand.

Entering Slovenia

Hills where the bears wander,

mountains into mist,

three bridges over the river.

Take the path through to

new light, in autumn air.

No one invited us here.

No one knows where we are.

We could drive south to Trieste, Venice or

disappear north over the next ridge.

It doesn't matter. It's not important.

The wind blows through us,

rests on the fur of the lynx and

blows away.

Vilenica

On the wall, the saints' eyes
are gone, the pigments believed
To cure blindness.

On the wall, the Devil,
just behind Jesus,
has Mussolini's face.

On the wall posters,
a niche with flowers,
the marks that bullets leave.

Above the walls,
the Slovenian moon,
not yet complete.

For Liudvikus

Amber in alcohol a resiny

sting on the tongue,

vodka on the move,

on the run –

coke in the strip bar,

downtown, rivers run

out of Russia,

to the sand sea of Nida.

Drinking with your father,

fifteen years in Siberia he

hands me a glass –

Dusk, and it looks like rain.

Vilnius, Lithuania

Lithuanian Prophecy

Maybe he said we were going

     to Kaunas, or Klepeda.

Maybe we had had

     too much to drink.

Maybe we ended up

     on sand beaches in Nida.

Maybe the river will stop flowing.

Maybe there will be amber.

Maybe the storks will come.

Maybe we were never

     really here at all.

Stork sky amber river

Inside the bear

there is snow and cold water.

Outside, storks fly north,

from the desert, bringing

good luck.

Everything comes to the river,

following a map of amber

ancient pine forests, resin flow,

rivermouth lagoon.

I will return,

encased in amber,

when the black storks

fly home.

Nida, Lithuania

CUBAN HEART

In 2004 Richard Lee and I traveled from Brunswick, Maine, to our sister city: Trinidad, Cuba, with a group of musicians, artists and poets. In Trinidad I spent time with the poets of the city: Ainsley del Carmen Mira Lladosa, Pavel Esquerra Diaz, Luis Martinez Ruiz, Pedro Juan Medina Dominguez, Hector Adonis Miranda Requera, Andres Cruz Rodriguez, and Manuel Alberto Garcia Alonso. Despite the many communication difficulties, Manuel and I have kept in touch, and have strengthened our connection through an ongoing linked poem.

You cannot embargo the human heart.

Poems marked gl are by Gary Lawless

Poems marked maga are by Manuel Alberto Garcia Alonso

Someone said to love your enemy.

Someone said Thou Shalt Not Kill.

Someone said to love your neighbor as yourself.

Someone said you can't go there but

Someone said to follow your heart.

Someone said it isn't possible but

Someone said it is and

Yes, it is.

gl

Here we are, in the hope and love of our friendship.

Here we are, with the sound inside our hearts.

Here we are, happy like the new world,

a world without darkness and fury.

Here we are, in the hands of love,

the sweet love of the earth.

Two countries,

and the air, and the fragrance,

and the smiles of justice.

Yes, my verses are all truth and joy.

maga

Eleggua opens the way,

gives us a good road,

a road of saints and spirits,

a way into this green land –

smoke and a prayer,

rum and a flower,

drum and a song –

a road of saints and spirits –

Eleggua opens the way.

gl

Notice

This is my life,

swift like the flowers,

and I never scream

in the middle

of the night.

I don't believe in fate.

I don't believe in coldness.

I don't believe in silences.

This is the party of the truth.

The truth coming with silence.

maga

I am waiting for a boat,

just offshore, stalled

in the fog –

a boat of revolution,

a boat of hope and joy.

I am waiting for the men,

long hair and beards, smoking

big cigars, who will

ride down from the mountain

on donkeys and mules.

I am waiting for whole

towns to rise up,

calling for justice, for liberty.

I am waiting for the courage

to step into my own life,

move toward the sound of

people singing, join them in

our walk to freedom.

gl

The revolution

at the edge of the fog

is a bleak, windy spot:

discovery,

reality and certainty.

People sing, translucent

as the light that sprouts

from the children.

I also wait,

slow in motion,

until my own freedom.

maga

Come down from the sky

down from the clouds into

a land of sun

a land where

old gods wear

the names of saints where

Eleggua gives you a strong welcome but

Ogun is your man, watches

over you, comes

to live in your house in

a dry iron altar of

old tools, horseshoes,

nails in a clay pot.

This is not

the island of heaven, this

island where spirits dance, where

the sky comes down,

enters your body and

lives in your heart.

gl

The Eternal Harmony

I have a dream :

the clear wind

the transparency of air,

the marvelous fragrance

 of the earth,

the friendship between

the caribou and the man,

the splendid silence

of the night,

the agreement

with the flowers,

the incredible

message of eternal harmony,

the eternal harmony,

the harmony...

maga

Sardine Shards

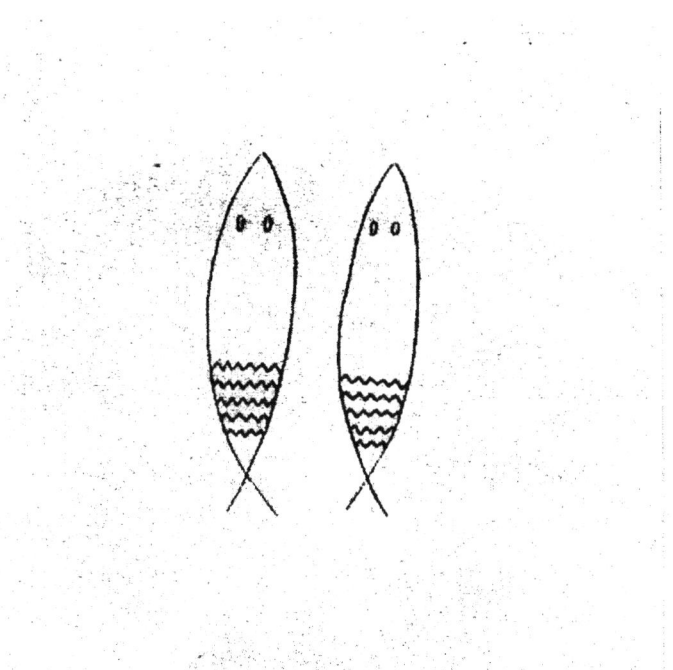

(sardine factory, Belfast)

May we be blessed by

the spirits of these fish

swimming through our world

from the world above

from the world below

rising from the depths of our future

blessing the depths of our past

Waited in the dark

In the dark they

gather in the cove

nets, in the water,

nets, in the morning

torn and gone, all gone –

Were there ever any fish?

Was there ever any sunrise?

Did we dream water full of silver our

pockets full of gold?

Falling into the soft

sea of darkness

slowly, slowly to bed

Wrap me in a blanket of fish

shining in the water like stars

like light from a million years

below some vast ocean of sky

where there is nothing

nothing to hold on to –

Flashes, flashes and then

Gone

I am calling the stars in to me

Come in through my head

Come in to my chest

Come in to my heart

Stars fall, become

shining fish

in my body, in my body

darkness falls, becomes

cold in my body

I am cold water

becoming fish

from hot stars

becoming granite

calling the water to

come into my body

Stars have fallen into the water

Stars have fallen into the rock

The sun enters the water

The moon enters the water

The stars enter the water

The light enters the water

Fish, shining like shards.

Sing a song of herring

all those sweet

sardines those

little fish those

flashes of light

in a dark world

bringing the world back

bringing the world back

to us

Migration Prayer

We will greet them with colorful flags,

wave them on their way through,

light fires, burn incense,

prepare a feast to say

"We wish you well,

pray for your travels.

Take care. Take care."

Listening For Loons

Recently I took part in Maine Audubon's Loon Productivity Study, here on Damariscotta Lake, then and again this year taking a two-hour paddle every three or four days to hang out with the loons, to see what they were up to, what was stressing them, if there were nests or young loons, to watch and listen and also to hang out with geese, turtles, osprey, eagles, beaver, lichen and other friends around the lake.

My friend the painter/poet Stephen Petroff says that he is trying to paint the contents of his heart. In a poem twenty years ago I wrote that, like loons, we sometimes "dive under/dive under and/come up somewhere else" These poems come from paddling, from diving under, from the loons, from my heart.

i

Wild roses down
to the water
One loon alone
northeast of the island
cedarscent

ii

bright daylily line
high on a hill
across the lake
oak breeze shoreline
trees, osprey
on Loon Island, again
watching, watching
loon calls
off to the east

iii

train whistle breeze

through trees and

beaver down no

loons around

iv

water lily or loon white

on the water both

bright

flowers flowers

on the surface of

this world

v

Loons take our love

into the lake

Hello hello

Which is the

real world water

in all this darkness

The loons calling

Goodnight goodnight

I love you

vi

every night now

I listen for loons

to hear their voices

to leave this body

to return to stars

vii

Last night, in the moonlight

at least three loons

voices in the distance

beyond the edge of darkness

viii

voices

through the night

through trees, fields

moon light

voices through moonlight

loon over

water through

the night

ix

to be in the company of

these trees, these grasses

these rocks, this water

these birds

hello hello we

finish each other's

sentience

x

siren on the highway

geese calling I'm

lashed to the mast

.

xi

pollen covered lake

three loons, together, these

holy places

behind the islands

xii

rockground north of the island

loons in sundown light

voices, across the water

wind blowing smoke

xiii

floating Deep Cove silence

we all dissolve, shimmering

and I learn that light

is alive

xiv

dragonflies, calm water, loons

you tear a hole in the world

take away the wind –

no words, there are

no words, just

water

xv

two loons, before twilight

slipping away, into night

turtlesplash

Chimney Farm

Chimney Farm

(June, 1987)

There is an empty stall in the barn where Ironside Jack the
stallion lived .Last week two Amish farmers and their driver
came and took him to Pennsylvania along with Sally the mare.
From Jack's stall in the barn you see the farmhouse:
weathered, red, and surrounded by flowers. Beyond the house
you look east over the horse pasture and down to the lake.
There are vegetables and wild lupine off to your right, and the
place where the town road ends. Near dusk the horses walk
to the fence gate, hoping for grain. These horses haul our
winter wood, turn the earth for our gardens. They give us
warmth and life .Jack was like the guardian spirit of the place,
always watching everything from here in his stall. Across the
lake, cottage windows reflect the setting sun. Birds fill the air
with sound. The light in the kitchen is yellow. Fog moves in
behind the islands and everything starts to quiet. Later the
loons will call from the cove. We will sleep, dreaming of
wind, of rain, horses moving in the barn, and loon song, loon
song pulling us into the dark water. We dive under, dive
under and come up, somewhere else.

Full moon eclipse

For Caryn

Wild things are howling.

The moon is gone.

Everything is shadows.

We lie on our backs, in darkness.

Friends disappear into the lake, come out

on the other side of the stars.

We look for them

in the Milky Way.

Congratulations.

Gradually, the light, returning.

Some clear night like this,

when the stars are all out and shining,

our old dogs will come back to us,

out of the woods, and lead us

along the stone wall to the cove.

There will be foxes, and loons,

a houseboat floating on the lake.

The trees will lean in, a lantern

swinging over the water, the creaking of oars.

Now we will learn the true names of the stars.

Now we will know what the trees are saying.

There is wood in the stove.

We left the front door open.

Does the farmhouse know

that we're never coming back?

This morning the field

is full of trucks,

tractor trailers with

pieces of a house soon

to stand where last year

there was forest.

This morning the turtle who

spent the week laying eggs

in the sand beside the road

lies crushed on the pavement,

eyes open, still breathing, and

just down the road,

the squirrel has already died.

These are the first signs.

We leave the earth a cleared place,

spaces where the woods were,

spaces where the turtles were.

What becomes of the world

with us in it.

I will move the beautiful bodies

into a woods of their own.

I will rest my head on the moss

in the secret place where the ladyslippers bloom,

where the deer bring me mushrooms,

where the granite heart of the earth beats,

where plant sway and needle drop

are songs on a sweet wind,

where love is what moves us all,

held close to the warm earth,

where we are at rest, at peace.

Head of the Tide

What is happening here?

Here where the gentle stream

murmurs its song,

on and on.

Here where sunlit leaves

turn in the breeze,

where stone walls and apple trees

look to the past and

the water, the water,

all the way to the bay.

Everything happens here.

Here where the mosses come

to tell their stories

resting on rock on

granite outcrop,

here where the kingfishers fly home

where hemlock breathes

where fern and iris rest

along the river.

Everything happens here.

Late and the light

stays, longer –

We wander the fields

count the stars

listen for loons -

If there is wind

we thank it -

carried away

Summer and friends

come and go.

We complain about

the tick, the blackfly,

horsefly and mosquito.

Still complaining as we

fill the wetlands, dry

the vernal pools, drain

the fen, lose

the scrub oak, fragile

places where

they begin to disappear.

Here are the names

we might never say again:

    Ringed boghaunter, katahdin arctic,

    Clayton's copper, pygmy snaketail,

    Twilight moth.

Summer is a long season

when you're never coming back.

Monarchs rise from milkweed,

head for Mexico,

Goodbye.

(Summer and friends…)

Someday we will

all be here alone or

Someday we will all be

here, together.

Ganoderma.

Every summer the tourists

rip the deep red mushrooms

from fallen hemlock and stumps.

Sometimes they carve their names.

Always they leave them to rot.

These same mushrooms, in Chinatown,

bring eighty dollars per pound,

Mushroom of immortality.

We cannot own these woods.

We cannot lay claim to the land.

He fell asleep, mushroom

in hand, dreaming of immortality,

flew above the trees, looking

down on his hut, his body, we

cannot lay claim,

even to that, the fruiting body

ripped from the earth,

dreaming of immortality.

She slept on the floor of

our cabin, dreaming of dolphins.

We drove north.

I have been looking for the animals

willing to talk with me –

in Newfoundland, the caribou –

in Alaska, the ducks –

on Isle Royale, the moose –

What will come of our conversations?

Better to know wind and water,

walk the woods and

navigate the stars.

For Preble Street

Sometimes the road keeps moving.

You can't just stand there,

you have to go with it –

Sometimes the road is a river,

under blue sky, winding

past the mountains, down

through the valley.

Sometimes there is a town –

and the river moves through it –

and we move through it like water –

smooth, fast, remembering

the cabin, the fire,

the open door,

and every goodbye we have said

to every place that ever mattered,

Sometimes the road keeps moving.

You can't just stand there.

You have to go.

In the heart where

all paths cross,

cross and move on,

where all that we

love connects where

what is best, within us,

flies

on this day when

birds choose their mates,

when love flies out

into the world, rises

sharp-eyed from

among the feathers –

We hang in thin air, fragile,

part of everything,

love the wind which

carries us,

love the path

in the heart where

all paths cross.

For Kate

Today the blueberries
taste like pine.
I look across the field,
to the cemetery, see
horses, running –
prayer flags
in the breeze.
Nothing is settled.
Smoke covers the hay.
We are waiting
for your call.

Caribouddhidharma

Caribouddhidharma came from the West,

riding on the back of a caribou.

He brought me sardines

packed in the ice of glaciers.

He told me that bears are gods,

that birds are songs.

He told me that plants

are great teachers.

He told me to listen to granite.

He left behind relics,

bones and bits of fur,

here in my heart.

Geese song, crow song

        Time to leave, time to go –

Geese song, crow song

        Time to leave, time to go.